DON'T GIVE UP... DON'T EVER GIVE UP®

The Inspiration of
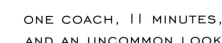
★ JIMMY V ★

ONE COACH, 11 MINUTES,
AND AN UNCOMMON LOOK
AT THE GAME OF LIFE

JUSTIN SPIZMAN & ROBYN F. SPIZMAN
FOREWORD BY NICK VALVANO

CHIEF EXECUTIVE OFFICER OF THE V FOUNDATION FOR CANCER RESEARCH

 sourcebooks

Published by Sourcebooks, Inc.
P.O. Box 4410, Naperville, Illinois 60567-4410
(630) 961-3900
Fax: (630) 961-2168
www.sourcebooks.com

Library of Congress Cataloging-in-Publication Data:

Spizman, Justin.
    Don't give up...don't ever give up : one coach, 11 minutes, and an uncommon look at the game of
life / Justin Spizman and Robyn F. Spizman ; foreword by Nick Valvano.
        p. cm.
    1. Valvano, Jim. 2. Basketball coaches—United States. 3. Life skills. 4. Success. I. Spizman, Robyn
Freedman. II. Title.
    GV884.V34S65 2010
    796.323092—dc22
    [B]
                                            2009039307

Printed and bound in China.
OGP 10 9 8 7 6 5 4 3

ACKNOWLEDGMENTS

Few, if any, accomplish something really important in life without the support of a team. Writing a book is no different.

There would be no book without the listening ear and confidence in our vision that Nick Valvano gave us from the start. He spearheaded this effort and helped it to become a reality. Thank you, Nick, for believing in this project and allowing us the honor of sharing the lessons learned from Jimmy's speech; and thanks to Bob Valvano for your time and wonderful stories about Jimmy, along with your helpful guidance. We are especially grateful to you both and The V Foundation for your meaningful support.

To Rosa Gatti of ESPN, who assisted us with the legal details and more, we are appreciative beyond words for your outstanding help, along with ESPN for its ongoing dedication to share the inspiration of Jimmy V and his legacy. To our devoted literary agent John Willig of Literary Services, Inc., who grew up in the same town as the Valvano family and was an enormous fan of Jimmy V. We thank you for your valuable guidance and persistence throughout this project. You embody the spirit of Jimmy V and we are privileged to work with someone with your insights. Thanks also goes to our editor Peter Lynch and the talented staff at Sourcebooks for believing in this book and recognizing the purpose and power behind Jimmy V's speech.

Jimmy V knew the importance of family, and it's no coincidence that a son-and-mother team coauthored this book. I wish to thank my wonderful mother for her endless support and meticulous attention to detail; I am your biggest fan. To my father, for always pushing me to be the best I could be, whether on the sports field or in my professional life. To my sister, Ali, whom I admire more and more every day as she grows into a beautiful and successful woman, and to Phyllis and Jack Freedman, John and Diana Milner, and our entire family who cheer me on at every turn.

To my beautiful bride, Jaime, thank you for supporting me when I needed support, and pushing me when I needed a shove. You are my best friend and I look forward to spending my life with you, because I truly have found someone I cannot live my life without. You light up my world and I love you.

And most importantly, my gratitude goes to the legendary giant of the man behind this book, Jim Valvano. None of this would have been possible without your powerful words and beautiful spirit. Also to Jim's entire family and group of supporters. You have created a rock-solid legacy for an amazing man who deserved it. Jim planted the seed, and you have tended the remarkable garden that grew. Thank you for your dedication to helping the fight against cancer.

And finally, to every person who has fought cancer, been touched by this illness, or is determined to help find a cure; with your support, we will beat this disease. "Don't give up, don't ever give up."

CONTENTS

FOREWORD

When I was asked to support this book, I had originally said that there are enough books written about Jim. I guess as the older brother I never really looked at Jim as a celebrity. During most of our early years, my job was to look out for my little brother. My friends were Jim's friends as he was included in all our games and activities. Since none of us really wanted him around, we made no concessions for his age. Jim began to show the traits that made him a successful player and coach, as he would always find a way to compete and many times beat the "big kids."

Over the years he continued to display a fierce competitive drive, a strong will, and an ability to make us all laugh. As he became success-ful, our family was thrilled for him, but I am sure none of us thought we were seeing anything exceptional. It was just Jim being Jim, competing, advancing his career, and making everyone laugh along the way.

All that changed in June of 1992 when Jim was diagnosed with cancer. From that moment on, all our lives changed. Although he was receiving the best care and advice, it became apparent that this was Jim's difficult opponent. He continued to be positive, and on every trip to the hospital for his treatment, Jim would visit with the other patients, and, as expected, the room was filled with laughter. For me, it made me angry and frustrated to see my brother being sick and there was nothing I could do to help him.

In January 1993, ESPN approached Jim and offered to help him start a foundation to fight cancer. Jim readily accepted and spent the next few months asking family and friends to join his last team as well as learning all he could about cancer research. As he did his whole life, Jim was trying to find a way to win.

The first ESPY award show was being held on Tuesday, March 4, 1993, and Jim was to receive the first Arthur Ashe Award for Courage. I was with him on the previous Sunday and asked about the show, the award, and should I cancel my business trip to Chicago. Jim said I should go on the trip since this was the first show, and he hadn't even decided what he was going to say when he received the award. Talk about a bad decision!

Jim's ESPY speech has become legendary. It gave America a glimpse of the courage needed to fight this disease and, for many, the lessons they can use in their daily lives. In my ten years as CEO of The V Foundation, I have heard countless times, from people of all ages, how listening to this speech continues to motivate them.

On behalf of our family and the Board of Directors of The V Foundation, I want to thank all of you for your support and generosity as we try to achieve Jim's dream of a cancer-free world.

—Nick Valvano

INTRODUCTION

O n March 4, 1993, Jim Valvano made history. He was honored with the inaugural Arthur Ashe Courage and Humanitarian Award at the first annual ESPY Awards presentation. No one knew it at the time, but the speech he delivered would make an indelible mark on the hearts of every listener. Less than a year before his famous ESPY speech, Jim was diagnosed with a rare form of cancer. He was part of just 2 percent of all cancer patients whose doctors could not figure out the origin of the cancer. Because of this rare situation, Jim's cancer was extremely difficult to fight. Doctors told him he had only a short time to live, and on the night of the speech, Jim was covered in tumors and could hardly muster the strength to make it to the stage to accept his award. However, even though he was in unbearable amounts of pain, Jim, known to millions of fans as "Jimmy V" delivered one of the most moving and courageous speeches that anyone has had the privilege to hear.

He didn't plan it that way; it's just who he was. The words he spoke in those eleven minutes contained powerful lessons on how to live a full and meaningful life. Years later, his inspirational message has survived the test of time.

At the time of the speech, Jim did not know the lasting effect his words would have, but he knew he had a message in his heart, which would hopefully encourage people to support an important cause. Since 1993, The V Foundation, founded by ESPN and inspired by Jim Valvano, has raised many millions of dollars to find a cure for cancer.

His inspirational message has survived the test of time.

After his speech, there was an outpouring of love for Jimmy V and a landslide of support for his cause, which has only gained momentum over the past fifteen years. While Jimmy V's life and valiant battle inspired people to give, the life lessons offered in the speech are inextricably linked to The V Foundation's core message. The V Foundation embodies Jim Valvano's spirit and commitment to making a significant difference and winning big in the game of life.

Jim Valvano gives us hope, and his speech continues to remind us of how one person's thoughts and desires can truly make a difference. His message was simple, yet profound. People facing challenges in life, from illness or other circumstances, need to continue daily to keep hope and courage alive. They need to embrace life to its fullest, focusing on the important things and letting the little things be exactly what they are…little things. Jimmy V taught us that living each day as if it were our last is powerful, and that each day is a blessing and each moment a gift. Cherishing life was at the core of Jimmy V's message; never forgetting that no matter what you face, either professionally or personally, "Don't give up, don't ever give up."

Sadly, Jim passed away fifty-five days after the ESPYs aired, but the speech and his legacy lives on through The V Foundation. It thrives through The V Foundation's dedicated supporters and the committed efforts of ESPN and the ESPY awards. Jim's dream has come full circle, building one of the most powerful and motivated organizations in the fight against cancer. The V Foundation provides cancer patients hope for a better tomorrow and the needed inspiration to fight this dreaded disease. Even in the face of challenge or tragedy, there is so much to live for and every day counts.

Don't Give Up…Don't Ever Give Up focuses on these life-affirming lessons and brings a call to action. If we listen carefully to what Jim said, we will all be better for it and gain strength and courage. Jimmy V's final wish was to continue to fight this battle even after his death. And with the creation of The V Foundation, he did just that. His dream of creating a force in the battle

Even in the face of challenge or tragedy, there is so much to live for and every day counts.

against cancer started small and has grown into a monumental tribute to a life well lived.

The lessons presented in this book are gifts. Jim gave us these gifts and it is our hope to pass on these gifts with the desire for you to implement these lessons into your own life. These lessons are food for thought, inspiration for the soul, and motivation for the mind. In the face of imminent death, Jim exhibited exuberant life. Jim did not view cancer as his fate, but rather as motivation to pack even more into his life and work even harder to achieve his goals. Jim lived his life to its fullest even before he got sick, but his sickness was just fuel for his fire. We hope Jimmy V's lessons fuel your spirit for life as well. It is our hope that this meaningful message lives on through the important work of The V Foundation, and that you will gain much from the powerful lessons in this book.

THE SPEECH

Jimmy V was a catalyst. He was a dreamer. And he served as an inspiration to so many. Facing his own mortality, he stood tall and found the courage and bravery for one last call to arms. He took the world's biggest stage and delivered some of the world's biggest lessons. These lessons were the heart of the speech, and the inspiration for this book. These lessons have lived on through Jim's legacy and the work of The V Foundation.

So, what exactly did Jimmy V say on March 4, 1993, at Madison Square Garden? What lessons did he present to the world that had such a lasting effect, which transcended generations, lifestyles, and beliefs?

It all started with a speech.

The following is a transcript of Jimmy V's ESPY speech from the Jimmy V Foundation's website. Please take this opportunity to view the attached DVD of Jim's ESPY speech.

Thank you, Thank you very much. Thank you. That's the lowest I've ever seen Dick Vitale since the owner of the Detroit Pistons called him in and told him he should go into broadcasting.

I can't tell you what an honor it is, to even be mentioned in the same breath with Arthur Ashe. This is something I certainly will treasure forever. But, as it was said on the tape, and I also don't have one of those things going with the cue cards, so I'm going to speak longer than anybody else has spoken tonight. That's the way it goes. Time is very precious to me. I don't know how much I have left and I have some things that I would like to say. Hopefully, at the end, I will have said something that will be important to other people too.

But, I can't help it. Now I'm fighting cancer, everybody knows that. People ask me all the time about how you go through your life and how's your day, and nothing is changed for me. As Dick said, I'm a very emotional and passionate man. I can't help it. That's being the son of Rocco and Angelina Valvano. It comes with the territory. We hug, we kiss, we love. When people say to me how do you get through life or each day, it's the same thing. To me, there are three things we all should do

Time is very precious to me.

every day. We should do this every day of our lives. Number one is laugh. You should laugh every day. Number two is think. You should spend some time in thought. Number three is you should have your emotions moved to tears, could be happiness or joy. But think about it. If you laugh, you think, and you cry, that's a full day. That's a heck of a day. You do that seven days a week, you're going to have something special.

I rode on the plane up today with Mike Krzyzewski, my good friend and wonderful coach. People don't realize he's ten times a better person than he is a coach, and we know he's a great coach. He's meant a lot to me in these last five or six months with my battle. But when I look at Mike, I think, we competed against each other as players. I coached against him for fifteen years, and I always have to think about what's important in life to me are these three things: where you started, where you are, and where you're going to be. Those are the three things that I try to do every day. When I think about getting up and giving a speech, I can't help it. I have to remember the first speech I ever gave.

You should laugh every day.

I was coaching at Rutgers University, that was my first job, oh that's wonderful [reaction to applause], and I was the freshman coach. That's when freshmen played on freshman teams, and I was so fired up about my first job. I see Lou Holtz here. Coach Holtz, who doesn't like the very first job you had? The very first time you stood in the locker room to give a pep talk. That's a special place, the locker room, for a coach to give a talk. So my idol as a coach was Vince Lombardi, and I read this book called Commitment To Excellence by Vince Lombardi. And in the book, Lombardi talked about the first time he spoke before his Green Bay Packers team in the locker room, and they were perennial losers. I'm reading this and Lombardi said he was thinking should it be a long talk, or a short talk? But he wanted it to be emotional, so it would be brief. So here's what I did. Normally you get in the locker room, I don't know, twenty-five minutes, a half hour before the team takes the field, you do your little x and o's, and then you give the great Knute Rockne talk. We all do. Speech number eight-four. You pull them right out, you get ready. You get your squad ready. Well, this is the first one I ever gave and I read this thing. Lombardi, what he said was he didn't go in, he waited. His team wondering, where is he? Where is this great coach? He's not there. Ten minutes he's still not there. Three minutes before they could take the field Lombardi comes in, bangs the door open, and I think you all remember what great presence he had, great presence. He walked in and he walked back and forth, like this, just walked, staring at the players. He said, "All eyes on me." I'm reading this in this book. I'm getting this picture of Lombardi before his first game and he said, "Gentlemen, we will be successful this year, if you can focus on three things, and three things only. Your family, your religion, and the Green Bay Packers." They knocked the walls down and the rest was history. I said, that's beautiful. I'm going to do that. Your family, your religion, and Rutgers basketball. That's it. I had it. Listen, I'm twenty-one years old. The kids I'm coaching are nineteen, and I'm going to be the greatest coach in the world, the next Lombardi. I'm practicing outside of the locker room and the managers tell me you got to go in. Not yet, not yet, family, religion, Rutgers basketball. All eyes on me. I got it, I got it. Then finally he said, three minutes, I said fine. True story. I go to knock the doors open just like Lombardi. Boom! They don't open. I almost broke my arm. Now I was down, the players were looking. Help the coach out, help him out. Now I did like Lombardi, I walked back and forth, and I was going like that with my arm getting the feeling back in it. Finally I said, "Gentlemen, all eyes on me." These kids wanted to play; they're nineteen. "Let's go," I said. "Gentlemen, we'll be successful this year if you can focus on three things, and three things only. Your family, your religion, and the Green Bay Packers," I told them. I did that. I remember that. I remember where I came from.

It's so important to know where you are.

You have to have a dream, a goal.

It's so important to know where you are. I know where I am right now. How do you go from where you are to where you want to be? I think you have to have an enthusiasm for life. You have to have a dream, a goal. You have to be willing to work for it.

I talked about my family; my family's so important. People think I have courage. The courage in my family are my wife Pam, my three daughters, here, Nicole, Jamie, LeeAnn, my mom, who's right here too. That screen is flashing up there thirty seconds like I care about that screen right now, huh? I got tumors all over my body. I'm worried about some guy in the back going thirty seconds? You got a lot, hey va fa Napoli, buddy. You got a lot.

I just got one last thing, I urge all of you, all of you, to enjoy your life, the precious moments you have. To spend each day with some laughter and some thought, to get your emotions going. To be enthusiastic every day and as Ralph Waldo Emerson said, "Nothing great could be accomplished without enthusiasm," to keep your dreams alive in spite of problems whatever you have. The ability to be able to work hard for your dreams to come true, to become a reality.

Now I look at where I am now and I know what I want to do. What I would like to be able to do is spend

The ability to be able to work hard for your dreams to come true, to become a reality.

whatever time I have left and to give, and maybe, some
hope to others. Arthur Ashe Foundation is a wonderful
thing, and AIDS, the amount of money pouring in
for AIDS is not enough, but is significant. But if I
told you it's ten times the amount that goes in for
cancer research. I also told you that five hundred
thousand people will die this year of cancer. I also
tell you that one in every four will be afflicted with
this disease, and yet somehow, we seem to have
put it in a little bit of the background. I want to
bring it back on the front table. We need your
help. I need your help. We need money for research. It may not save my life. It may save my
children's lives. It may save someone you love.
And ESPN has been so kind to support me in
this endeavor and allow me to announce tonight,
that with ESPN's support, which means what?
Their money and their dollars and they're helping
me—we are starting the Jimmy V Foundation for
Cancer Research. And its motto is "Don't give up,
don't ever give up." That's what I'm going to try
to do every minute that I have left. I will thank God
for the day and the moment I have. If you see me,
smile and give me a hug. That's important to me too.
But try if you can to support, whether it's AIDS or the
cancer foundation, so that someone else might survive,

Cancer can take away all my physical abilities. It cannot touch my mind, it cannot touch my heart, and it cannot touch my soul.

might prosper and might actually be cured of this dreaded disease. I can't thank ESPN enough for allowing this to happen. I'm going to work as hard as I can for cancer research and hopefully, maybe, we'll have some cures and some breakthroughs. I'd like to think, I'm going to fight my brains out to be back here again next year for the Arthur Ashe recipient. I want to give it next year!

We can learn a lot from the words of Jimmy V.

I know, I gotta go, I gotta go, and I got one last thing and I said it before, and I want to say it again. Cancer can take away all my physical abilities. It cannot touch my mind, it cannot touch my heart, and it cannot touch my soul. And those three things are going to carry on forever.

I thank you and God bless you all.

These were the words of Jimmy V's now legendary ESPY speech. At the time Jim stood in front of the star-studded audience, he did not know what he was about to create. He knew he had a cause and he knew he had a dream. But little did he know his dream would become a legacy of remarkable proportions.

The legacy of Jimmy V is not only seen through the creation of The V Foundation or through every dollar of the more than $90 million The V Foundation has raised for cancer research but also through the words of Jim and the lessons we can use in our daily lives.

We can learn a lot from the words of Jimmy V. In fact, he articulated seven lessons in his 1993 ESPY speech. As we will explore, each one of these lessons will offer a succinct and powerful way to change your life. They will motivate you, inspire you, and hopefully touch your heart in a meaningful way.

– Cherish Time, Treasure the Moment
– Make a Habit of Wild Enthusiasm
– Think, Laugh, and Cry
– Live the Big Picture
– Out-Dream Yourself
– Believe in Something Passionately
– Don't Ever Give Up

CHERISH TIME, TREASURE THE MOMENT

Time is very precious to me. I don't know how much I have left and I have some things that I would like to say. Hopefully, at the end, I will have said something that will be important to other people too…I urge all of you, all of you, to enjoy your life, the precious moments you have.

—Jimmy V

As Jim was standing in front of the audience at Madison Square Garden on that fateful night, the moment was frozen in time. Time was precious to him that night, because he had little time left. And as he stood taking this moment in, Jim was about to make history, almost ten years after he first became a household name.

Ten years earlier, Jimmy V was the coach of the 1983 North Carolina State University Wolfpack collegiate basketball team. On April 4 in Albuquerque, New Mexico, Jim's NC State Wolfpack was facing the University of Houston Cougars in the NCAA tournament championship game. Jim's team was a heavy underdog. But with a basketball coach like Jimmy V, you could imagine he had other plans. Jim's team was not going to listen to the media and the analysts who said they had no chance. And they would not stop believing or fighting for the title, no matter how tired or exhausted they were, at least not if Jimmy V had anything to say about it.

NC State entered the tournament as a low-ranked seed and expectations were not high. The Cougars were favored to win the championship from the beginning of the tournament. They were a powerhouse and significantly outmatched Jimmy V's team.

But Jim believed triumph was possible in the face of defeat.

To the total amazement of almost everyone watching the game, with just seconds on the clock, the score was tied at 52. Coach Valvano's team had already done more than anyone thought they would. In the eyes of the world, they had done enough. But as the old adage goes, "It is not how you start, it is how you finish." And these boys had some finish in them. With ten seconds left, Dereck Whittenburg lofted a high-arching shot from thirty feet out. The shot fell short of the rim and landed in the waiting hands of Lorenzo Charles. Charles exploded to the rim and dunked the ball as time expired. Final score: NC State, 54; University of Houston, 52.

Triumph was possible in the face of defeat.

As the final horn sounded and NC State upset the University of Houston, a man rose from the sidelines and frantically ran throughout the court looking for someone to embrace. He jumped in the air with clear enthusiasm on his face. This man just orchestrated history. He had built his team, taught them, educated them, and pushed them to levels they never thought they could achieve. Like the director of a spectacular film or the orchestrator of a beautiful symphony, this coach had created a work of art, a history-making squad. This was one of the greatest moments in sports history and one of the biggest upsets in college basketball history. Remembered as a triumphant moment in time, year in and year out during every NCAA tournament thereafter the image of Jimmy V running around the court and jumping in the air enthusiastically has become a billboard of sorts for the exuberance and excitement of March Madness.

Like the director of a spectacular film or the orchestrator of a beautiful symphony, this coach had created a work of art, a history-making squad.

As the horn blasted, Jim Valvano ran onto the gym floor on April 4, 1983, in Albuquerque, New Mexico, and right into the history books.

Ten years later. March 4, 1993. New York, New York. Madison Square Garden.

Jim Valvano was sitting backstage at the inaugural ESPY awards, an Oscar-like award ceremony hosted by ESPN for the sports world. Weak, tired, and covered with cancerous tumors, he was a man who was hanging on by a thread. Less than a year before, he was diagnosed with cancer. Shortly after, he found out that the cancer had metastasized. He had undergone brutal treatment, taken endless amounts of medicine, and faced this battle like any battle in his life: head on and with a positive attitude.

He was fighting the greatest battle of his life, but somehow, someway, he fought through the agonizing pain and suffering so he could be backstage, waiting to hear his name called, ready to accept the Arthur Ashe Courage and Humanitarian Award.

Legendary sportscaster and Jim's friend Dick Vitale said,

As I reflect on those moments, the memories come flooding back. I flash back to Jimmy standing up there after struggling to get on the stage. I figured he would simply say thank you. He could barely make it to the podium, yet he electrified the audience with a brilliant speech. The crowd in the house and the TV audience heard something they will never forget—Jimmy V was at his best. He rocked the crowd. I was stunned watching him, with the crowd in the palm of his hand as he poured his heart out about battling cancer.

On that night in Madison Square Garden, Jimmy V changed the face of cancer research. He announced the creation of The V Foundation to help fight the disease that afflicted him and so many others. In just eleven minutes, Jimmy V laid the groundwork for raising more than $90 million for cancer research, and inspired hundreds of thousands of people to give, to participate, and to fight together in hopes of beating this terrible disease. Jimmy V orchestrated another storybook ending on that fateful evening, but this time it was a chapter for each of us to share and define for years to come.

Yet as Jimmy V addressed the audience and poured out his heart, he also noticed a light indicating how much time he had left. Jimmy could not help himself, and quickly said, "That screen is flashing up there thirty seconds like I care about that screen right now, huh? I got tumors all over my body. I'm worried about some guy in the back going thirty seconds? You got a lot, hey *va fa Napoli*, buddy. You got a lot."

Va fa Napoli is Italian for "go to Naples"—slang for "get outta town." That simple phrase encompasses so much of Jimmy V's character. Even when he was gravely ill, tired, worn out, and fighting for every word, he could still cherish the moment, and in the midst of this emotional and difficult speech, Jimmy V recognized the moment and instinctively took the opportunity to deviate from his speech and let his character shine through. As he stood on stage, he not only urged us all to live life to its fullest, he stood there as an example as well. It is easy to talk the talk, but Jimmy V will always be remembered not only as a big talker, but also a big walker. Jimmy V always backed up his words through actions and results.

———

Do any of us really know how much time we have in this world? Moments are precious. The hands of time are always moving. When you are young, you think you are invincible. You think you have all the time in the world. But life is short and moments are fragile. They quickly become memories as we each move through our own personal journey. Yet, we eventually learn we are not immune at any age. The sooner we accept that, the quicker we are on the road to what a good life looks like. Jimmy V died too

He not only urged us all to live life to its fullest, he stood there as an example as well.

young. But during his life, he accomplished so much. And he did so through living life to its fullest and cherishing every moment.

It's clear Jimmy V was special not just because he enjoyed his life and cherished his time after being diagnosed with cancer, but, rather, Jimmy was remarkable because he lived his life that way even before he knew his days were numbered.

Nick Valvano, CEO of The V Foundation and Jim's older brother said,

Moments are precious. The hands of time are always moving.

Jim taught others to enjoy life. I think he had a rare trait. People listened to him and believed in him. When he spoke, he was not speaking down to someone. He made people look at themselves. He was a celebrity, but he was not a movie star. Rather he showed the world he was a regular guy who puts his pants on one leg at a time. That's a talent and that is why that speech is still so important years after he gave it. It is still so important because of who Jimmy was. People connected with Jimmy. People all the time come up to me and say, "I met your brother at a speech he gave and after listening to him for five minutes I felt like I've known him all my life." And then people would change a little something about their lives based on what he would tell them while speaking.

Jim is an example of someone who understood the word *cherish*. Not only when he was standing in the face of cancer did he cherish what mattered most, but even years prior he embraced life with a respect for every minute. When you cherish something, you hold it close and you hold it tight. That is what Jim did with his life.

Jimmy V had a miraculous gift he gave to others young and old alike. In 1986, after Jim's Wolfpack team defeated Navy in a close game, Jim and his coaches went to a local bar. Lesley Visser, a famous sports journalist and the first female beat writer for the NFL, remembered Jim's love for life and his ability to cherish every moment fondly.

After the victory, everyone celebrated at a local bar. Jim had everyone within fifty miles singing the praises of the Wolfpack. Somehow, dancing broke out and, of course, Jim was in the middle of it. Right then was what I loved about him most—he didn't care if you were young or old, black or white, rich or poor—everybody was invited. On this night, he was dancing with someone's grandmother, the happiest eighty-year-old you've ever seen—and I'm sure she felt twenty years old inside. Such was the miracle of Jim Valvano.

Moments like this are what made Jim so special. Moments like this are what made the Jimmy V blueprint so useful. Every moment we have the opportunity to sing and dance. Or we can sit in the corner and watch everyone else light their lives on fire. Jimmy V had a special way of lighting his own life on fire. Time is precious and there is always a chance to ignite the world, and Jimmy V always took that chance to infuse his life and the lives of those around him with happiness and enjoyment. There is no mystery to the equation, only opportunity. And the best part is you have control over every opportunity that presents itself. You can always choose to cherish the moments and light your life on fire, just like Jimmy V did.

***

Every moment we have the opportunity to sing and dance.

So what does this have to do with you and the rest of us? People spend so much of their lives regretting and carrying anger and frustration with them. Forgive easy and have a short-term memory, because when you hold negative feelings toward people, you aren't enjoying all life has to offer. You are focusing on the negatives, and you will surely lose sight of the most important things in life. Life has a way of giving you its nectar one beautiful moment at a time. A long embrace with a loved one, a gorgeous sunset outside your home, watching your children grow up and become successful adults, or even just sitting down for a second and thinking about how lucky you are to be healthy and alive. Life gives you the opportunities to appreciate it, but it is your job to wrap your arms around these opportunities.

When it is all said and done, if you can reflect on your life, and with a confident breath say that you have enjoyed life, you have not only done yourself justice, but you have been a gift to all the people around you. Enjoying your life helps others enjoy their own. Jimmy V loved his life, and through his teachings and desire to view every moment as a precious opportunity, he made other people better for being around him.

Jim taught others to focus on today and enjoy their own lives much like Jim enjoyed his life. Nick Valvano says,

> During Jimmy's entire illness and after the speech, he used to always tell me, "Listen, Nick, you're the older brother and you better stop and take a look at your life and get a better balance in it so that you don't keep looking for the future. Find today and make the most of it." That changed my life and seeing someone you love go through an illness like that makes you think about what you do every day and what the value of what you do every day is. That's what Jim's ESPY speech tells me.

Enjoying your life helps others enjoy their own.

You have the same opportunity every day you are alive. Be enthusiastic, enjoy every day you have in front of you, and make the most of life's gifts, because as Jimmy V reminds us, life is in the details and little gifts arrive often. We just have to seize their presence and unwrap each and every one, including those not visible to the eye.

MAKE A HABIT OF WILD ENTHUSIASM

Cancer can take away all my physical abilities. It cannot touch my mind, it cannot touch my heart, and it cannot touch my soul. And those three things are going to carry on forever.

—Jimmy V

Enthusiasm is inspiration. When we see someone act enthusiastically, we are immediately drawn to them. And that is part of why Jim's speech is so special. When you have the opportunity to watch Jim's ESPY speech, you cannot help but feel drawn to his enthusiasm. Even in the face of Jim's sickness, his enthusiasm could be felt through his speech. We focus so much attention on what Jim said on that evening, but how he said it was just as important. Whether you attended the speech, watched it at home, or read it later, there is no doubt that Jimmy V's enthusiasm compelled your interest and grabbed your attention.

Enthusiasm is inspiration.

Not one word encompasses the persona of Jimmy V more than *enthusiasm*. Jimmy was immensely enthusiastic, and because of his constant excitement, everyone around him felt and acted the same way. The great thing about Jimmy V was you never knew what would happen next. The only sure thing was that Jimmy would be excited about what was happening, and you would share in his excitement and enthusiasm right there with him.

When we are enthusiastic, we tip the odds of succeeding in our favor. Half the battle is deciding our attitude wherever we are in life. Life is often unpredictable and you may have little control over plenty of aspects along the way, but you choose your attitude and how you react to situations and people. Choosing to be enthusiastic will help you deal with tough situations and manage challenges more efficiently.

Jimmy V faced one of life's most challenging tasks with a positive attitude. Cancer was his opponent, but he chose to be enthusiastic about his situation and inspired one of the strongest battles against cancer. When one person is courageous, it gives us all the inspiration that makes us feel like we, too, can rise to that challenge. Today, Jimmy V's enthusiasm has sparked the fight against cancer with the support of so many amazing individuals, including his family and even people Jim never even met.

True enthusiasm spills over onto others. That was another lesson that Jim's life embodied with extreme passion.

Bob Valvano remembers Jim's enthusiasm for life.

True enthusiasm spills over onto others.

Jim looked at life and challenges in a very special way. He always felt you could take a bad situation and make it really bad or you could take a bad situation and make the best of it. That's what made Jim special. He always found a way to be positive and enthusiastic about whatever situation he faced.

Jimmy V's enthusiasm made others feel special and welcomed. He was not just enthusiastic about his own life, but also about the lives of others. It did not matter what you did for a living or who you were, Jimmy was interested in you and your story. No matter what the scenario, Jimmy always had a lively interest in other people.

One day Jim was coaching a nationally televised basketball game against the UNLV Rebels. In the middle of the game, while one of his players was shooting free throws, he walked up to the scorer's table and sat down on it. No one had any clue what he was doing. He stood there for a minute, on a nationally televised game, and had a conversation with Joyce Aschenbrenner, the assistant athletic director for UNLV at the time. The producers and directors of the broadcast kept calling Aschenbrenner's phone to see what was happening and why Jimmy V was talking to her. The referees walked over and asked if everything was all right. Jim told them he was fine and the referee ordered him to his bench. It turned out that Jim asked Aschenbrenner a series of questions about her childhood and upbringing, after finding out Aschenbrenner grew up in Pittsburgh. As Jim walked away, he turned to Aschenbrenner and said, "Just wanted to make sure your mother back in Pittsburgh got to see you on national television." He then walked right back to his bench and continued stomping the sideline and throwing his hands in the air in his usual animated version of coaching. To this day Aschenbrenner says, "The Rebels won that game by six, but my mother became a big Jim Valvano fan."

This is just one beautiful example of Jim's view of life and his ability to make people around him smile and share his enthusiasm. He expressed his own enthusiasm for life by shining the limelight on others. Even when he was in the stress of a nationally televised game with thousands of people in attendance and millions watching on television, he just could not help his enthusiasm for someone else's life shine through.

When you ask how someone is, listen. Listen with your heart and soul, not just your mind.

Being interested in someone else was a gift he possessed. It ultimately made people feel special and is something we can all do daily. When you ask how someone is, listen. Listen with your heart and soul, not just your mind. Look for opportunities to give. Then decide, what are you going to do about it? What can you do to make a difference? That is the Jimmy V way.

This was the case when Jimmy V gave his riveting speech in 1993 at the ESPY awards. Jim was standing on stage, fighting for his life, and yet he could not help but be wildly enthusiastic. For many people enthusiasm is a choice, and Jim always chose that path.

Jim's blueprint for life was fueled by enthusiasm. Even when you are facing the most difficult situations in life, as Jimmy V was when he gave his famous speech, try to let your enthusiasm shine.

What was so moving was that Jim's enthusiasm was injected into his every day life. When we choose to do something for long periods of time, it can often become a habit. That was why Jimmy V's enthusiasm was so special. It was not planned or scripted, but it was something he practiced, and like any great coach, practicing something until you are great at it is the key to success.

His basketball team may have lost a tough game, but he would be enthusiastic that the bus to take them back home arrived an hour early. Jim may have had a bad day of chemo, but he was happy that his friends were waiting for him after treatment to talk basketball. And finally, Jim may have been facing terminal cancer, but he could not prevent his enthusiastic view of life to take advantage of the moment to inspire the audience. As he was giving his speech and talking about enthusiasm, he was exuding more enthusiasm than anyone thought a man in his position was capable of. But that was just Jimmy being Jimmy.

Jim's older brother Nick remembered how Jimmy always looked like he was having so much fun in everything he was doing. He made other people feel good through his enthusiasm. When you feel good about yourself, you do good things and become successful. Jim made everyone around him feel good. When people would come to one of his clinics, they said they would be there just so they could go wherever Jim was. They said he would entertain them. They would go to these clinics just to be able to go to dinner or grab a drink with Jim afterwards. Jim's fun was contagious. People want to be around you when you are that alive and it also makes people listen to you. If he's having so much fun, you say to yourself, "I should lighten up and take things differently."

And that is the lesson Jim taught his audience on that faithful evening in 1993. Make enthusiasm a habit, not a choice. Nobody wants to be around a person who is negative and unenthusiastic. We are drawn to people who are intriguing and live their lives to the fullest. Exuberance, Excitement, Energy, and Enthusiasm: the four E's. If you walk around and habitually deliver the four E's, people will be drawn to you and your energy. Living your life with enthusiasm will not only draw people to you, but you will also be a gift to those around you, infusing their lives with happiness. Your enthusiasm will be contagious.

Linda Bruno, Jim's former administrative assistant at Iona College, articulates Jim's enthusiasm perfectly when she says,

Make enthusiasm a habit, not a choice.

Just before the season was to start, Jim burst into the office screaming inaudibly about something. This was not completely out of character for him, but he was

waving a magazine and pointing at a particular page. He raced around the office and it took almost a full minute for the staff to realize the reason for this outburst. For the first time in its history, Iona College basketball was ranked in the Sports Illustrated poll. While we all cried, Jim raced out of the office, down the stairs and out onto the track which circled the baseball field, at the center of the campus. Jim held the Sports Illustrated above his head and began doing laps around the track. As people stopped to watch, he yelled the good news, while he kept running. Soon a large crowd gathered around the field while Jim waved his arms excitedly, running with the magazine above his head the whole time. I looked around at the gathering crowd. Many were those that only a few months earlier thought that Jim's style might not be suited for Iona. They all began to applaud as Jim continued around the track.

If you focus on injecting every moment of your life with unlimited enthusiasm, you will see monumental changes.

Needless to say, when Jim found out about his team's accomplishment, he was overjoyed. He was excited, and he could not contain himself. But what made Jim's reaction so special was his enthusiasm. He was so over the top that he inspired a schoolwide reaction as well. Jim's enthusiasm was simply contagious. It could not be contained, and it spread like wildfire. Before Jim's reaction to the news ended, he had an entire stadium of fans rooting him on and standing beside him, all because of his contagious enthusiasm.

Make enthusiasm a habit and, in the Jimmy V tradition, an every day occurrence. Cherish every moment you have. Time is precious, and if you focus on injecting every moment of your life with unlimited enthusiasm, you will see monumental changes in your attitude and the attitudes of those around you. The four E's are like magnets. They will draw people close to you without them even knowing it. They will be attracted to your personality and won't even know why. All they will know is that they like to be around you and respect your passion and enthusiasm for life.

LESSON 3

LAUGH, THINK,
AND CRY

To me, there are three things we all should do every day. We should do this every day of our lives. Number one is laugh. You should laugh every day. Number two is think. You should spend some time in thought. Number three is you should have your emotions moved to tears, could be happiness or joy. But think about it. If you laugh, you think, and you cry, that's a full day. That's a heck of a day. You do that seven days a week, you're going to have something special.

—Jimmy V

Back when Jim was a young child, Nick Valvano reminisces, Jimmy used to show up at his brother's classroom, burst in, and do his best impression of Jimmy Durante. An American icon, Durante made people laugh for decades; apparently, Jimmy V considered Jimmy Durante a namesake and, naturally, mimicked him. Of course, while Nick's classmates would be hysterically laughing, he would instantly sink down in his own chair. Jim would start singing and dancing while the teacher was in the middle of a lesson. Jim was only in the third grade, but he knew even then that the power of laughter was contagious, and any opportunity he had to make people laugh was simply a priceless moment.

That was the beauty of Jimmy V. When he coached his players, he followed his own lessons: to laugh, think, and cry. In Jim's ESPY speech, he told everyone listening to laugh, think, and cry. And after Jimmy V was done making the crowd at Madison Square Garden laugh, he also made them think. In just minutes, he gave the world his three rules of life and since then, as his words live on in perpetuity, the world has taken his advice to heart.

Laughter makes the world go round. The more you laugh, the happier you will be. And Jimmy V knew that and lived life out loud. He felt that laughing was one of the three most important things that you could do each and every day. Listen to a good joke, laugh about a funny story you heard, or just laugh to laugh—whatever the case, it is good for the heart and therapeutic for the soul.

Laughing is like medicine for the sick, strength for the weak, sunshine for the dark. Laughing, if only for just a few minutes, makes you forget the stress in your life and focus solely on what you are doing... laughing. Laughter is infectious, so when you laugh, make sure it is loud and boisterous. Because when people see you laugh, it has a magnetic effect. They are drawn to you and immediately smile and want to know, "What's so funny?"

The more you laugh, the happier you will be.

Laugh hard. Do it every day, and not only will people want to surround themselves with you and your boisterous happiness, but they will all be better for doing so. And if at any moment you do not have anything funny to say, laugh at yourself.

Jim never took himself too seriously and even during his ESPY speech, he kicked it off with humor. After he was introduced by the legendary sports commentator, Dick Vitale, he looked down at the crowd, and his first words were, "That's the lowest I've ever seen Dick Vitale since the owner of the Detroit Pistons called him in and told him he should go into broadcasting." Even knowing the seriousness of the situation, Vitale could not help but laugh at the joke and sigh at Jim's timeless sense of humor. He started one of the most serious moments of his life off with a joke. And guess what? It cut the tension and intensity of the moment and the crowd began laughing, too.

If you have the opportunity and the ability to make other people laugh, it is not only your job but your responsibility to do so. Because we are better for laughing and you do a service for your friends, family, and loved ones by making them laugh. Laughing allows you to express your inner happiness in a very outward manner. It is a tunnel to your heart and an expression of your innermost feelings. When Jimmy V started his speech at the ESPYs, he started with a joke. Guess what? Everybody laughed with him. And for that, he made everyone in that room, if only for a few seconds, happier. If Jimmy V can laugh and tell jokes in the face of cancer, then can't we all just laugh at the small trials and tribulations we face in life?

Bob Valvano says,

> *I remember when Jim was sick. People would always call him. The funny thing is the reason why they called may have been to see how he was doing and try to make him feel better, but I think in the process, Jim made them laugh and they felt better by the end of the call.*

Laughter is infectious, so when you laugh, make sure it is loud and boisterous.

The second thing Jimmy V said to do every day is to think. Jim believed that "a mind is a terrible thing to waste." Think about the capacity your mind has when you really apply yourself to a situation; think about how easy it is to solve a problem, or come up with a brilliant idea. Your mind is one of your strongest tools and resources, and the more you use it, the sharper it becomes. Since we all can only hold one thought at a time, Jimmy V used the power of his mind each and every day of his life in a meaningful and beneficial manner. He knew cancer would inevitably take many of his physical abilities, but it could never take his mind away and his ability to think. So he thought and thought and thought. He thought how his battle could inspire others. And he thought how his experiences could help others. And he thought how, even if he lost his battle, he could do something to help others beat cancer.

Thinking is quite possibly one of the easiest things to do on a daily basis.

Jim was a scholar of life. Nick Valvano remembers that Jimmy never read a fiction book after college. He would always read autobiographies or nonfiction. He was blown away by authors like Thoreau and Emerson and could not help but quote them and study them on countless occasions. Jim wanted to be the best, so he studied the most inspirational "thoughtprovokers" on earth. He admired these authors and spent as much time as he could thinking about their lessons and their teachings.

Ralph Waldo Emerson once said, "The ancestor of every action is a thought." Jim never stopped thinking. His dream of creating a successful and influential organization to help in the fight against cancer started when ESPN approached him and proposed the creation of The V Foundation. This thought fueled his dream and if you can think big, then you can surely dream big.

Thinking is quite possibly one of the easiest things to do on a daily basis. It does not cost any money, does not take up much time, and you really do not have to exert any physical ability. You are always with your thoughts, and you can always find a few minutes to think about something. You can use your mind at work on a challenging project, or use your mind at home, perhaps to think of a creative way to teach your children to read and write, or even use your brain to teach your new puppy to sit; your mind is a powerful tool that benefits so many people, including you, when you use it.

A little bit of thought goes a long way.

So take a few minutes each day of your life and think. Think hard. Think long. Break your thinking down into one take-away action at a time and take action. A little bit of thought goes a long way. We are so fortunate in life to be given the ability to reason and face life's challenges with a sharp and finely tuned mind, but when we react without thinking, we miss the opportunity to do great things. Just think what thinking can do.

"You should have your emotions moved to tears."

Those were the words of Jimmy V, his third thing to do each day. He knew the importance of being emotional and being moved to tears every day of your life. Showing emotion makes you human. It is one of our most defining qualities. Holding things in and allowing them to eat you up from the inside out is unhealthy and detrimental to your growth as a person. But sharing your emotions in constructive ways is very liberating to your mind, body, and soul.

Showing emotion makes you human.

Now I know what you are thinking: "If I am too emotional, people will think I am just that, too emotional." If you are lucky enough to see something or feel something that brings you to tears, you have had a pretty fulfilling day. That seems to be what moved Jimmy V—being moved to emotion. Whether it is a beautiful picture or an emotional song or even a funny movie, the experiences that bring us to tears are by far the most important experiences we can have in our lives, ones that turn into memories.

Shortly after Jim won the 1983 championship, he and his brother Nick paid a visit to a camp for children who were battling cancer. Nick says Jimmy would never be quiet, but during the tour of the camp, he was completely speechless. After the tour, Jim turned toward his brother and, with tears streaming down his face, said, "Nick, we have to do something about this." Shortly after and for years to come, Jimmy would always work to raise money and pay visits to sick children. The tears on that day inspired Jim to help others. The emotional strain on Jim's heart when he saw those sick children pushed him to make a difference long before he himself was diagnosed with cancer. Jim always felt tears were the lubricant of success. They can guide you and push you toward making change for the better, and in this situation, Jim's emotions motivated him to help those children he met on that day.

Wake up every day searching for that one thing that will elicit an outpouring of feelings.

Emotion is a therapeutic way to release your feelings. They help you heal, they allow you to grow, and they motivate you to find exactly what you love in life and surround yourself with it forever. If you see something that elicits a reaction of intense emotion, you know, right then and right there, that is something you should be around. Because life is about loving and being emotional, and emotion is a reaction to an overflow of feeling. So be emotional and wake up every day searching for that one thing that will elicit an outpouring of feelings.

Think about this analogy for a moment. Tears are like pressure. You feel them building up and you feel the emotion beginning to run through your body. The pressure builds, and it feels like the weight of the world is on your back. You do not fight it and you begin to start crying. You cry long and hard and tears roll freely from your glossy eyes. And then it happens. You begin to pull yourself together, you wipe the spent tears from your face, and you take a deep breath. The great part is after this short experience, you might even feel better. The problems may not instantly disappear, but you discover that even though life is fragile, you can work your way through the tough times.

Sometimes you have to cry because of pain, but many times you have the opportunity to cry tears of joy or tears of emotion. Tears of joy are tears that fall because of the happiness you are experiencing. Tears of emotion may be reactionary tears, like tears that fall because you are watching a heartfelt scene in a movie. Tears are nothing more than an intense and heartfelt emotion. Jimmy V taught us in his speech to not fight our emotions. He believed that emotions are natural and human and the only way to live is to embrace whatever emotions arise. Emotions are not scripted and you cannot plan when you will laugh or cry each and every day, but if you embrace the opportunity to do so, you will surely live a full and enjoyable life.

Jim did not necessarily mean for you to shed water like a broken pipe every day, but rather, to embrace your emotions and never hide your feelings. Emotions are natural. Everyone has them, but not everyone embraces them. And that is sad. Exhibiting emotions makes you human. They show you care and allow people a better opportunity to understand who you are through seeing what you care about. Emotions are the common denominator among us all, so why not embrace such a vital characteristic of our existence?

———·———

We are lucky if we have the chance to laugh and think and cry. Some people do not get to laugh every day. Too many people do not spend enough time in thought. And finally, rarely do enough of us exhibit pure and intense emotions each and every day. Many times we sell ourselves short on life by pulling back. It is like riding a horse. If you are about to take a jump and you pull back, you will fall off the horse or hit the obstacle you are trying to clear. But if you go full speed ahead and embrace the jump, you will successfully clear your obstacle.

Embrace the emotions that present themselves and do not pull back.

The same is true in life. Go full speed ahead. That is the only way to do it. Embrace the emotions that present themselves and do not pull back. If you do, you will lose a valuable opportunity to laugh, to think, or to cry. There are so many instances to exhibit all of these emotions, but so many times we overlook these opportunities because we are too concerned with what others will think. Who cares if people are laughing with you or at you, so long as everyone is having a good laugh?

Laughter, thought, and tears are absolutely free. They don't come with a price tag and will not take away from the mortgage, or the groceries, or any other bills. Just think about it. We spend so much time complaining about the possessions we do not have when, in reality, God gave us three of the most valuable opportunities in life and did not charge us a thing for them. Rich or poor, laughter, thought, and tears won't cost you a penny. So invest less time in complaining about what you don't have and more time appreciating what you do have, because the price tag of not laughing or thinking or crying is one you cannot afford to pay.

Laugh. Think. Be moved to tears. Jimmy V did it every day of his life. And because he did, he lived an immensely fulfilling life and it did not cost him a thing.

Laugh.
Think. Be
moved to
tears.

LESSON 4

LIVE THE BIG PICTURE

I rode on the plane up today with Mike Krzyzewski, my good friend and wonderful coach. People don't realize he's ten times a better person than he is a coach, and we know he's a great coach. He's meant a lot to me in these last five or six months with my battle. But when I look at Mike, I think, we competed against each other as players. I coached against him for fifteen years, and I always have to think about what's important in life to me are these three things: where you started, where you are, and where you're going to be.

—JIMMY V

Jimmy V never lost sight of what was important in his life no matter what he faced. He dedicated his life to something bigger than himself. Even when diagnosed with cancer, he knew he had a bigger cause, and he refused to let himself become a victim. He was going to live his life on his own terms. And so, he focused on the big picture. He knew he had a higher calling, and with his thoughts and his dreams and his drive, the big picture presented itself: finding a cure for the sickness that would eventually take his life. Jimmy V did not sweat the small stuff because focusing energy on things that did not matter took energy away from the things that really did matter, like family and friends.

We tend to get upset about the little things.

Jimmy V reminds us to stop and look at the big picture. Take a moment and think about where you stand in life and where you would like to be. The old saying goes, "Sometimes, you can't see the forest for the trees." Meaning, at times, we are so close to a situation and so involved we can't look at it in a "big picture" sort of way.

We then focus our energy on things that really don't matter. There are things in life that are worth getting upset about. But more times than not, those things are not what upset us in our daily lives. We tend to get upset about the little things, like traffic, or a long line, or a stain on our shirt. In the big picture, these trite occurrences don't matter, but we seem to assign them some importance. You are lucky to own a car and sit in traffic, or to be able to stand in a long line or afford your nice shirt. Just think about how many people there are in this world that would give anything to have any of those mishaps happen to them.

You have to save your energy for the big things in life.

If you allow, the small things will just chip away at you and wear you down. You have to save your energy for the big things in life because, when they come, you are going to need it.

Focusing on the big picture is looking at the end result as your goal and staying the course, not losing track of where you are, but focusing on where you want to be. This will keep you on track and allow you to maintain a high level of desire to achieve exactly what you want to achieve, no matter what bumps and bruises you may experience along the way. Jimmy V knew his course and knew what he wanted his end result to be, and through the inspiration of his words and the hard work and generosity of family and friends, his dream came true and his big picture is now a reality. Jimmy V found a meaningful way to live on even after his death and make his life count.

Every day of your life, reflect on the three time frames Jimmy suggests: where you started (the past), where you are (the now), and where you are going to be (the future). The three time frames work wonders for your attitude and will allow you to see exactly what parts of your life need improvement and what parts are right where they should be.

———

Begin every day and think about exactly where you started.

Where did you come from? What positive life experiences have you had? What negative life experiences have you had? What have you learned from your mistakes? What lessons have you learned from your success? These are all vital questions to ask yourself when trying to understand where you started your life. Once you understand where you started, you will understand why you are the person you are.

Growing up, Jimmy V's father always told him that he should be kind to the people he passes on the way up because he will see them again on his way down. Jim treated everyone with dignity and respect and never forgot where he came from. Bob Valvano remembers the uniqueness of the procession line at Jim's funeral.

You would see Coach Dean Smith, sports commentator Digger Phelps, and then in between the two of them, you would see the cashier at Wendy's who just got off of his shift. That was the type of guy that Jim was. It did not matter who you were. He would treat you the same way, and he never forgot his roots and what our parents taught us.

It's important to understand your roots. You can never forget where you came from and you always have to remember that your past made you who you are today. Jim embraced his past throughout his entire life. He was proud of his heritage, his family, and his city. And he respected those who helped him and in turn he helped others. He wore his past on his sleeve and was always happy to talk about growing up in Long Island. When Jim began getting grants and raising money for scholarships, he insisted that money go directly to helping people get a start. He remembered when he was young and Bill Foster (a friend and former coach) gave him his start in coaching as the freshman men's basketball coach at Rutgers. Jim never forgot that it all started with one man believing in him and giving him a chance.

You can never forget where you came from.

———————

Jim very much lived in the moment. He always felt you should know where you are in life. During his ESPY speech, Jim was motivated by the cancer that was spreading throughout his body. He knew his days were numbered and his time was limited. And he embraced the situation.

When he won the championship in 1983, he knew his success had reached an all-time high. So what did he do? He used his position to make a difference in the lives of others. He coached harder, took more pride in his job, and reached out even more to those that were in need of his help. And then, ten years later, he knew cancer would eventually take his own life, but he also knew he had the opportunity to help others who face the same challenging situation.

During one of Jim's final interviews he stated, "I want to help every cancer patient I can now. I don't know if I can handle that, but it's the only conceivable good that can come out of this."

This is one of the most important lessons to learn from Jim's speech. Know where you are and take advantage of that to dictate exactly where you plan to go. If you understand where you are in your life, you can then set achievable goals and plot out your pathway to achieving those goals. Jim felt life was as much about positioning as it was anything else. At the end of the day, we are all in different positions in our own lives. Some may be content with where they are, some may want to improve their positions, and others may feel they need to change their position for whatever reason. However, once you understand where you are in your life and what is and is not controllable, you truly can begin to understand where you are headed.

Every day of our lives, we should wake up and ask ourselves, "Am I happy with exactly who I am and where I am?"

Jim had an amazing ability to always appreciate and value where he was at the time, but simultaneously look to the future in hopes of making a difference and reaching his personal goals and desires.

Pam Valvano, Jim's, wife said,

Every day of our lives, we should wake up and ask ourselves, "Am I happy with exactly who I am and where I am?"

When Jim Valvano was seventeen years old, he took out a simple white index card and wrote down all of his professional aspirations. He would play basketball in high school and college, become an assistant basketball coach, then a head coach, achieve a victory in Madison Square Garden, and finally cut down the nets after winning a National Championship. Jim's ability to see his place in the world with such clarity was truly a gift. This simple card, coupled with a strong belief that he could control his fate, would guide the next ten years of his life. At the age of 36, Jim could take out his tattered index card and cross out every single dream.

Once Jim was diagnosed with terminal cancer, he knew exactly where he had to put his energy. He immediately knew he had to raise money and spread the word to the best of his ability. And he did just that. Because of his life experiences and his ability to face challenges and conquer them, he was able to embrace his current situation and plot his future course. Jim could have lay down right then and there and bowed out respectfully in his fight against cancer, and no one would blame him for it. But Jim was a fighter. He was a fighter in 1983 in that famous championship game, and he was a fighter in 1993 when he was battling cancer. Jim was destined to make a difference, even against insurmountable odds because he knew where he was going.

We have that opportunity as well every day of our lives. Look at your current situation and make a list. Let's call it the "ten-year plan." Just like Jim, who had a tattered index card with his ten-year plan, do the same. Write down ten things you would like to achieve in the next ten years. Whether it is to be a better cook, receive a promotion, or spend more time with your children, jot them down. And then tuck the list away and revisit it often through the ten years, crossing off each one of your accomplishments and filling in that line with a new potential achievement. This will allow you to annually review your life. It will also allow you to always be working on at least one way to improve who you are and where you are going. One step at a time.

In 1983, after defying significant odds and running across the basketball court looking for someone to embrace after winning the national championship, Jim had no idea

Write down ten things you would like to achieve in the next ten years.

he would be fighting a very different set of odds ten years later. Then in 1993, when he was speaking to a theater of thousands and a television audience of millions, he offered a simple and powerful list of lessons he lived his life by, but had no idea where his message and efforts would be in ten years. He knew he had to take advantage of every day he was given, and he knew he had to remember where he had been, where he was at the moment, and where he wanted to be in ten years.

You should always be your biggest fan and your most difficult critic.

Now, a little more than fifteen years after Jim lost his battle to cancer, look what his ten-year plan has accomplished. Look at how Jim practiced the lesson know "where you were, where you are, and where you are" and realized his opportunity to help others. He wanted to start an organization to help in the battle against cancer. And he announced he was doing so in 1993 during his ESPY speech. Since then, The V Foundation has raised $90 million and counting to find a cure for cancer.

Jim taught us a lot in just eleven minutes at Madison Square Garden. But this lesson was the foundation for all of the other lessons in life. Always start from the beginning and never forget where you came from. Think about where you are in your life at this moment in time. Consider your strengths and weaknesses. Assess yourself and decide what you would like to personally improve.

You should always be your biggest fan and your most difficult critic. Give yourself credit where credit is due and be tough on yourself when need be. Rethink what you do every day of your life and be open to living your life different ways. Finally, spend some time every day thinking about where you want things to be in ten years. For now, in the moment, figure out your position and figure out where you want to go. Plot your course because only then can you start heading toward your destination.

OUT-DREAM YOURSELF

To keep your dreams alive in spite of problems whatever you have…You have to have a dream, a goal. You have to be willing to work for it.

—JIMMY V

George Bernard Shaw once said, "You see things; and you say, 'Why?' But I dream things that never were; and I say, 'Why not?'"

Jimmy V was a lot of things. He was a basketball coach, a sports commentator, a husband, a father, and a friend. But more than anything, Jimmy V was a dreamer. He dreamed open and often. He was happy to speak to anyone and everyone about his dreams. Whether it was a dream he had the night before, or a future dream to create a more harmonious basketball team or a successful philanthropic organization, dreaming was part of Jim's every day life.

But it was not the fact that Jimmy dreamed that made him so special, it was the way in which he dreamed. Jimmy V did not believe in small dreams. He did not believe in small thoughts, because small thoughts produce small results. What made Jim Valvano so special, among other things, was his ability to out-dream himself. He reached high and dreamed big, because only big dreams create big opportunities.

It was clear even in his final days that Jim never stopped dreaming. Even in the end, Jim knew he was fighting an unbeatable battle. However, his dream was to make sure that his battle was not for nothing. He wanted to make sure that while he may lose his battle, he could give others a better chance to win their own.

A big dreamer is not created overnight, but rather, is an individual who has been shaped and molded through years of perseverance, hard work, and dedication to a cause. Dreamers back up their thoughts with actions. It is easy to wake up one morning and scream to the skies that you are going to dream big. Easier said than done, to say the least. The best way to fully understand how to dream big is to look at those people who have successfully done so themselves. To be the best, sometimes it is essential to study the best. And Jimmy V was one of the biggest and brightest dreamers we have ever seen.

A big dreamer is not created overnight.

Speaking about Jim's ability to dream, Bob Valvano says,

The older I got the more I realized what a special gift Jim's ability to dream was. I think he had this ability because Jim never really worried about not making it. If he dreamt it, he expected to achieve it. That is just the way he was.

When Jim started coaching at Johns Hopkins, it was more known for its academics than its sports program. The basketball team had a long way to go, but you would never know it by Jim's attitude. When Nick Valvano called Jim at the start of the first season he coached at Johns Hopkins and asked him how they were going to do this season, Jim immediately replied, "Nick, we are starting two gynecologists, a surgeon, and two cardiologists. Who could beat us?" This was the way Jim thought. He may have been a jokester at times, but he was a dreamer all of the time. He dreamed big and never settled for anything less than the best, no matter what the circumstances were. He expected the best out of people and, more often than not, got it.

It is important to challenge yourself on your journey through life. Out-dreaming yourself is one way in which you can do just that. If you dream big, you are essentially setting the bar for yourself very high. The old saying goes, "If you shoot for the moon and miss, you will at least be amongst the stars." Many people are scared to dream big for fear of failing. But ask yourself, what's the worst that can happen? If you do not reach your dreams, the mere process of dreaming and working toward your dreams will be more fulfilling than you could ever imagine. If you dream big, even if you fall short of your dream, you may find that you have accomplished more than you ever thought you had the ability to accomplish.

It is important to challenge yourself on your journey through life.

While it is important to dream and recruit people for your dream through a positive attitude, dreaming without action is not dreaming at all. You must always support your dreams by actions. Dreams are great on paper, but they will not come alive unless you put the hard work and effort into them. A dream is much like a garden. It needs nourishment and attention or it will simply die. You cannot just plant the seeds for a dream. You must also water it and make certain it gets the necessary attention every day to ensure it grows into a beautiful flower.

You must always support your dreams by actions.

Jim knew how to make a dream become a reality. Whether it was the 1983 championship game or the 1993 ESPY speech, Jim had a very special formula. To make a dream a reality, it takes equal parts thought, passion, and diligence. It is that easy. Just like a garden calls for sun, water, and attention, your biggest dreams can come true through thought, passion, and diligence.

When dreaming big, it is important to think. What exactly is the purpose of your dream? What is the goal of your dream? How can you create a smart game plan to put your dream into action? What obstacles will you come into contact with while trying to make your dream a reality? How much will your dream cost you, both financially and personally? Once you can answer all of these tough questions, you will be ahead of the game and will give yourself the opportunity to see how realistic your dream really is. You may find you cannot afford your dream or do not have the personal time to achieve it. That is okay. It just means you have to wait for the right moment to put the ball in motion or attempt to rethink your game plan to better fit your lifestyle and your limitations. Jimmy V never let obstacles derail his dreams. Even when he passed away shortly after the creation of The V Foundation, he had already made the arrangements and laid the groundwork to ensure The V Foundation would be a success.

Passion for your dream is like gas for your car.

Once you figure out the blueprint for your dream, it is vital to put your heart into it. No dream has ever become a reality without a strong belief system.

Passion for your dream is like gas for your car. It makes it go. It powers it. Without you, your dream would be stranded.

Jimmy V was a passionate man and his passion for life was infused into his dream. He could not help but show how much he believed in his battle against cancer, and he showed it at every turn of the corner. During his ESPY speech, he knew he was close to reaching his goals.

He could feel it. He had the support of ESPN and an audience of thousands ready to join his fight. But what really made The V Foundation a success was Jim's passion for his cause and the steadfast support of his family and a group of believers. You could not help but want to be a part of his dream. And there lies the importance of infusing your dream with passion. If you believe in it and cannot contain your excitement about your dream, when you run low on gas, there will be plenty of others standing right next to you with a full tank ready to power your dream to reality.

While a dream needs thought and passion to become a reality, without action behind the meticulous planning and a strong belief in your dream, you will have nothing. You can talk about it forever and the whole world can be excited about your passion for your dream, but without action, your dream will be nothing more than a noble thought on paper. You have a blueprint for your car and you have the gas to power it, but eventually you have to hop in the driver's seat and put the pedal to the metal.

Yes, Jimmy V's life was cut short. But everyone who knew Jimmy agrees he felt he never got cheated one day of his life. That's a man who reminds us how precious each day can be and that we are all larger in some way than our days here on earth. We only have the present, which is a gift, and we don't know what tomorrow will bring, but to Jimmy every day was an opportunity to make a difference and live life to the fullest. It's the days of our lives, no matter how short or long, that add up to a life well lived.

When I asked Nick Valvano what Jim's biggest obstacle was in life, he immediately responded that Jim hated the fact that he had to sleep. Jim felt sleep prevented him from doing something special. He hated that he had to waste time sleeping every now and again. This defines Jim's work ethic and clearly shows why so many of Jim's dreams came true. He worked hard, never stopped moving his feet, and filled his time with action.

No matter what you do, if you do not work hard, then you will never succeed. However, on the flip side of that, if you do work hard, anything is possible and anything you imagine can come to life and become a reality. Jimmy V noted in his ESPY speech, "the ability to be able to work hard for your dreams to come true, to become a reality" is vital. Throughout his life, Jimmy V always exhibited a strong work ethic and always knew the value of hard work. Rome was not built in a day and neither will your big dreams. So it takes hard work and dedication to your beliefs and your ideas. You can think big, you can dream big, but if you do not work big, you are missing one of the most essential elements to finding success.

Rome was not built in a day and neither will your big dreams.

Now, working hard can come in many different forms. You can work through pain, or you can work long hours, or you can work smart, but no matter how you work, you have to remain dedicated to your cause and diligent in the process of reaching it. While hard work is just one part of the equation for success, it may in fact be the most important part.

The V Foundation is a result of Jimmy V's hard work and Jimmy V's unwavering dream. It is a product of his legacy and the hard work of thousands of people who are dedicated to Jimmy V's cause and Jimmy V's dream. Without his hard work during his life, The V Foundation would not be what it is today. Cancer research takes hundreds of thousands of hours and millions and millions of dollars, so if it were not for the hard work and efforts of all these people, many of whom were inspired by Jimmy V, The V Foundation would not be the driving force it has become.

So whenever you think big and you dream big, do not fall short in the effort category, because sometimes all it takes is a little diligence and dedication to a cause to turn that cause into a success. Why fall short on your dreams because you did not want to work hard to achieve them? Your hard work could change the lives of many people, so you owe it to them to think big, dream bigger, and work harder.

What if Jimmy V was not the hard worker he was? What if he did not work hard to prepare his team in the 1983 NCAA championship game? And what if he did not work hard and stay focused on his cause and his dream? Where would we be today? Lucky for us, we do not need to imagine a world without Jimmy V's hard work, because his hard work changed tens of thousands of lives for the better.

Jim was known for his actions as much as his reactions. He always had something to say and he illustrated that quality when he gave his ESPY speech. He was always coaching and was more than willing to offer some insight or a helpful hint he learned along the way. But more than anything, Jimmy V was about the action. He backed up his words with production and action.

Kay Yow, former NC State women's basketball coach and hall of famer, who sadly passed away from cancer in 2009, remembered Jim's prowess for action. After being diagnosed with breast cancer in 1987 and going through surgery, she received a phone call at home. It was Jimmy. He said, "Hello this Jim, what are you doing? My staff and I would like to bring you lunch today." She was weak and tired, but he insisted. He said, "Don't worry. When we get there just show us where everything is and we will set it up. We are going to come over, bring you lunch, and cheer you up." Well, he came over with almost the entire menu from a local Italian eatery. And they all ate and talked and took Coach Yow's mind off of things. She said,

There will be obstacles and struggles and frustrating days, but you cannot give up.

Just to have the thought to do something like that is special. I know basketball coaches and the schedule that a basketball coach and an athletic director has is very busy. There is an overwhelming amount of time spent and to take two hours out of any day with your entire staff is something extraordinary. It takes a special person just to think about doing something like that to begin with. Then follow through with it.

Action speaks louder than words. Dream big, believe in

your dreams, lay a strong foundation for them, but do not underestimate the importance of working hard to ensure they come to life. There will be obstacles and struggles and frustrating days, but you cannot give up and you must keep working toward your goal.

Thought, passion, and hard work: those were the lessons of Jimmy V. That was how he fulfilled his big dream. And the best part is, you have the same opportunity to fulfill your dream if you think about it, believe in it, and work as hard as you can to make it a reality.

BELIEVE IN SOMETHING PASSIONATELY

When you have a goal and when you have a dream and when you have a belief, and you throw in that concept of never stop believing and loving each other, then you can accomplish miracles.

—Jimmy V

Jimmy V was a believer. He felt that whatever you believe in, no matter what it is, you should stand strong and not waver in your beliefs. A belief system gives you hope and inspires you to think big and dream big.

Your belief system is one of the strongest tools you have at your disposal, as it is a guiding light that motivates you and defines what is important to you. Once you believe in something, you can begin to work to achieve it. Once you understand your belief system and choose to stand for something, the rest of the pieces will fall into place.

Jimmy V knew that believing gives you hope. It offers you something to aspire to and something to work toward. And if you believe strongly in your ultimate goal and want to show up for something larger than yourself that benefits others, people will want to be a part of your mission, whatever that is in life and at work. People are drawn to great ideas and enthusiastic individuals spearheading those ideas.

Once you believe in something, you can begin to work to achieve it.

Throughout history, those are the people who make us believe we, too, can do something great.

———·———

Jimmy V dreamed of starting a philanthropic foundation to raise money for cancer research. Clearly he never knew how big his dream would actually become, but most likely he wouldn't be surprised. When ESPN asked him if he wanted to start a foundation in his name, he could see into the future the possibilities. He was a visionary thinker and knew what should be done. He would have celebrated the donation of every single dollar to the foundation, large or small. He was fortunate that he had a strong legacy and support system to implement his dream and nourish it every day until it grew into what it is today. That was what made Jim so special. Even when he was facing terminal cancer, he mustered the strength and courage to deliver his riveting ESPY speech and believed he could help in the battle against cancer. And people from all corners of the world rose to support his dream, and they began to believe that finding a cure for cancer was possible.

Bob Valvano says,

When Jim was diagnosed with cancer he always said he had two choices. You can choose to live or you could wait to die. Jim chose to live and he believed that through his efforts and his work, he could make a differ-ence. And because of his belief, his dream is becoming a reality.

But more than anything, Jim's dream became a reality because he be-lieved in it with all his might and today that belief stands tall and proud.

He had a conviction with all of his heart and soul that through his determination and dedication to this cause, he could inspire others to perpetuate this dream. This is just one example of a belief system that was carried on by caring and the compassionate force of strength and hope. Jimmy V always believed in something. He was given a greater mission in life and chose to take it on with his entire being in the hopes of making life better for someone else. Jimmy felt strongly that you had to believe in something, no matter what it may be.

When Jimmy V was in high school, he was a three-sport star. He dreamed of excelling in three sports, believed he could, and worked to achieve that goal. Twenty years later, that philosophy—dreaming, believing, and working hard—made him a success again. He was a believer. It took some ability, and some intellect, but also, somewhere inside, Jim had this incredibly intangible capacity and drive to succeed and not fail. He applied that to everything he did. Nick Valvano says,

Jimmy V always believed in something.

> Whether it is a football, basketball, baseball player, coach, going into broadcasting, trying to do interviews, sideline reporter, no matter what Jimmy did, he just motivated himself to get the best out of him. When we started playing golf together, we would be

playing a round and he would hit a bad shot and just start talking to himself. I would hear him say, "You're an athlete; you can do better than this." He'd be talking to himself saying, "You can do better." Jim loved to compete, but more than anything, he believed in himself and that prevented him from ever failing. Those are the ingredients for a successful person.

———————

When Jimmy V believed in something, it was contagious. You could watch him speak about The V Foundation and he would light up. He could not hide his passion and sincerity for the cause. When he was diagnosed with terminal cancer, the first thing he told his doctor was that he was going to raise as much money as possible to fight the disease that would eventually take his own life. And when he received the Arthur Ashe Award at the ESPYs and gave his riveting speech, he spoke of the creation of The V Foundation. He took his moment in the spotlight to help others. His deeply rooted hope for a better world was cemented in time at the ESPYs, and the message of a healthier tomorrow for others living with cancer was clear.

Jimmy V made others want to dream with him. If he was willing to fight cancer under his own personal circumstances, why wouldn't they want to? This lesson is extremely important. It is not just a matter of what you believe in; it is a matter of how you go about making it happen. Dreaming big is important, but believing in your dream with every fiber of your being is what sets it in motion. Setting the goals of your dreams high are important, but recruiting others through your passion paves the way for a dream come true.

Jimmy V jump-started his own dream through his dedication and passion. He was the inspiration behind the foundation. But if it were not for his loved ones and ESPN standing right there beside him and supporting his goals, those goals never would have become what they are today.

Today, The V Foundation, run by Jim's older brother Nick Valvano, consistently has the support of ESPN, led by George Bodenheimer, and a wide assortment of friends and celebrities ranging from Jim's college teammate Bob Lloyd (chairman of the board for The V Foundation) to legendary sportscaster Dick Vitale and Coach Krzyzewski from Duke. And the reason why each one of them supports The V Foundation is easy to understand. It is because each of these individuals strongly believes in Jim's dream and being on his team. This doesn't take place on a court, but it's the ultimate game, the game of life, and the desire to help others.

Recruiting others through your passion paves the way for a dream come true.

Even today, we see how Jim's belief system lives on through the efforts of The V Foundation. Nick Valvano spoke of the board members at The V Foundation by saying,

Most of the people on the board of the foundation from the beginning are family, or now personal friends to us

and it's no different than any group of friends who lose someone they love. They came together. They were first motivated by grief and anger because they have lost someone and they want to do something. The V Foundation has an amazing engine of people who started that foundation and have been able to take those talents and things they bring to the foundation and start something remarkable.

They are still with us and that really is special. They were the apostles of sorts.

———•———

So what do you believe in? Sometimes belief means having faith in your-self and your abilities to solve a problem or achieve a specific goal. Other times, a belief may be your ability to trust someone to complete a task, which you asked him or her to take care of. A belief system comes in many forms, shapes, and sizes, but no matter what the scenario, if you believe, you will more likely have the shot to achieve. You always want to be an enabler in your beliefs and hope that they become a reality. If you believe in your goals and your abilities, you will enable others to do the same. And with that, you will gain support and dedication for whatever you believe in.

Gandhi once said, "Men often become what they believe themselves to be. If I believe I cannot do something, it makes me incapable of doing it. But when I believe I can, then I acquire the ability to do it even if I didn't have it in the beginning." Put in other words, this is the Jimmy V way: If you believe, you can move mountains. If you do not believe, you cannot move pebbles. Half the battle is the belief that you can succeed. No person has found the success they were looking for without first believing that they could achieve it and then practicing and working harder than necessary to get it right.

That is where your road to dreaming, success, and achieving all of your goals begins: with belief. Besides, why would you even consider taking on a task if you did not believe you could do it? What good would that do? Even if you do complete the task, I can promise you it will not be as good as it could have been if you believed in yourself.

If you believe in your goals and your abilities, you will enable others to do the same.

In 1983, facing an uphill battle, Jimmy V's NC State Wolfpack pulled off one of the biggest upsets in sports history. Most people did not believe they could do it. Thousands of people were convinced there was not a chance the game would even be close. But there was one man, his coaching staff, and his team that believed they could do the impossible.

Before the Houston game, Jim told everyone who would listen that his team would be just fine. When the NC State Wolfpack stepped on that basketball court in 1983, you can bet they believed they could beat the University of Houston. By the time the first half ended, their belief was turning into a reality and every person watching the game began changing their tune very quickly. Every last one of them was thinking to themselves, "Could they really do this?" And it all started with the belief of Jim and his basketball squad.

When you have that "always trying to find a way to win attitude," instead of the "I'm not going to lose attitude," you become creative and do things that other people would not do. If you tell yourself there is a way to win and I will find it, instead of focusing on the obstacles that can beat you, you will find yourself ahead of the game. That is what made Jim so special. He believed in his abilities and his players. Many coaches would not do what Jim did because they were worried about losing. Jim became known as one of the best bench coaches in college basketball. There wasn't anything he would not try. And he instilled that in his players as well. Every team takes on the personality of its coach. So Jim's teams were believers. They believed in their ability and they believed in one another. They trusted Coach V and always had the attitude of "I will find a way to win."

Why would you even consider taking on a task if you did not believe you could do it?

And guess what? After Jim's team beat the University of Houston, Jim received a letter from the legendary coach John Wooden, who won ten NCAA championships in a twelve-year span at UCLA. Coach Wooden told Jimmy that the 1983 championship game was one of the best-coached games he had ever seen.

Fast-forward ten years. Most people who knew Jim's circumstances did not even believe he would be able to make it through the ESPY broadcast. They thought they would hear a simple heartfelt thank you from Valvano after being honored for his humanitarian efforts. But Jimmy V had other plans. He believed he could find the strength to accept the award. He knew this was an opportunity to be the start of something very special. His belief that he could get through his ESPY speech propelled him and, in the end, everyone was right there with Jim and believed that the battle against cancer was a battle worth fighting for.

To this day those believers live on through donations and support for The V Foundation. Jim believed in his cause, and it was a call to arms. Today, tens of thousands of people from all walks of life give to The V Foundation and believe in Jimmy V and his dream. And to think it all started with one man believing in his ability and refusing to just say "Thank you for this honor."

So now the question remains: What can you do to achieve what you believe in? Every day you wake up, ask yourself, What can I do to achieve my beliefs? And think to yourself how you can answer that question. The answer may not come easy and probably will require some deep thought, but nothing has ever been accomplished

What can you do to achieve what you believe in?

without thinking about how to do it. Jim always asked himself how he could achieve his goals. Whether it was winning a big game or raising as much money as he could for cancer research, Jim always strategized and considered a plan of attack. He always thought about the steps he had to take and the obstacles he had to overcome. There was never action without thought and once action began, he did not stop until he achieved what he was shooting for. You have that same ability, but it is up to you to consider how to achieve your goals and to never give up.

DON'T EVER GIVE UP

Don't give up, don't ever give up.

—JIMMY V

The final lesson from Jimmy V's ESPY speech is the last line he passionately uttered: "Don't give up, don't ever give up." These bold words are perhaps the most important Jimmy V said on that memorable day. In fact, they are the easiest way to sum up Jimmy V—those seven words.

No matter what the situation, no matter how difficult the challenge and no matter what the odds, "don't give up, don't ever give up."

These words encompass everything that Jimmy V stood for and believed in. He was talking to every individual facing cancer or any other life struggle, focusing on their own personal challenge or life's ups and downs. He envisioned an outpouring of giving and the coming together as a team as any great coach would do. He gave the greatest pep talk of his entire career.

His big dream, his endless enthusiasm, his dedication and hard work, and his battle against cancer were all fueled by his fire and desire to never ever give up, no matter what the circumstances were. Success is often defined by how hard you work, but achieving your goals is certainly defined by never quitting. You have to be hungry for your dream and you have to overcome whatever obstacles you face.

Jimmy V could not be a better example of an individual who would never give up. He was simply unstoppable. In the face of adversity, whether it was an unbeatable basketball team or an incurable illness, Jimmy V never gave up and fought until he could fight no longer. He gave it his all, and even though he lost the battle against cancer, no one could ever say it was because he gave up.

As Jimmy closed his speech he said, "I know, I gotta go, I gotta go, and I got one last thing and I said it before, and I want to say it again. Cancer can take away all my physical abilities. It cannot touch my mind, it cannot touch my heart, and it cannot touch my soul. And those three things are going to carry on forever."

You have to be hungry for your dream.

If we learn nothing else from Jimmy V's life and the final game he "coached" at the ESPY awards, we must take to heart and learn that no matter who you are, no matter what you are faced with, and no matter how hard or how challenging it seems, "don't give up, don't ever give up."

During his lifetime, Jim had plenty of opportunities to throw in the towel. In 1983 when he was coaching against an "unbeatable team," or in 1993 when he was diagnosed with terminal cancer and told he had less than a year to live. Even on that night in 1993 when he gave his riveting speech, most people don't know that he almost did not attend the ESPYs that evening. He was sick and weak and did not think he had the energy to attend, much less give a speech in front of thousands. But Jimmy pulled it together, gritted his teeth, and when the lights went on and his name was called, as Nick Valvano put it, "All his aches and pains just went away."

Jimmy V was a fighter; in fact, he was a warrior. He never gave up and he never gave in. This was the way he lived his life. He faced every obstacle with the attitude of "how can I get through this?" He exhibited a constant level of perseverance, which was prevalent in every facet of his life. There was never the word try, only do.

Don't give up, don't ever give up.

One of Jim's favorite thinkers, Ralph Waldo Emerson, once said, "A hero is no braver than an ordinary man, but he is brave five minutes longer." That is just how Jim was. He just never gave in. He would reach as far as he could to get the job done, and if the job was incomplete, he would figure out a way to reach just a little farther. Jim always found the courage to be a little braver for a little longer. When he received his ESPY award for his courage in the face of cancer, he could have just said thank you. But that is what made Jim so special. He always found a way to win his fight and increase his perseverance and extend his bravery.

Bob Valvano says,

When I heard Jim's ESPY speech and I heard the words, I thought it was so simple. Don't give up, don't ever give up. I thought it was so obvious. But then I rethought the message and it was brilliant. Jim knew that you couldn't control certain things in life. In the end it was the perfect message, it was what Jim did for a year while fighting this illness. You can't control the cards you are dealt, but you have complete control over your own efforts and how you deal with the situation. And that is one of the most important things we can learn from my brother.

At one time or another, your life will throw you a curve ball. Maybe even a few. In fact, few of us really escape them along the way. It may not be fair, and it may come out of nowhere, but in that moment, you have two choices. One choice is to give in and give up. It is the easy thing to do. You won't have to fight and you won't have to be courageous, and it will be what it will be. However, the other choice you have is one that Jimmy V would tell you to take. Fight. Persevere. Don't quit. That is the way to fill your life with special moments. That is the way to overcome challenges and face obstacles. That is the Jimmy V way.

In his poem "The Road Not Taken," Robert Frost said, "I took the one less traveled by / And that has made all the difference." At the end of the day, you will be defined by the choices you make. More times than not, the right choice will not be the easiest. It may hurt more or take longer or challenge your character unlike anything else. But if you succeed and you get through it, that will make all the difference in the world. When diagnosed with terminal cancer, many people are struck numb by the terrible news. They are devastated and do not take advantage of the little time they have left. But not Jimmy V. He immediately knew he had the opportunity to make a difference.

When ESPN offered to help Jim and his family start a foundation in the battle against cancer, it was an easy yes. Jimmy had just been diagnosed and in the first ninety days of this disease his family was consumed with trying to educate themselves about what could be done. Jim was told he had eight or nine months to live and 2 percent of people with his diagnosis made it. Jimmy said, "Let's go find out what that 2 percent did to make it through this." As his family looked into the numbers, they quickly realized it was going to be difficult to win.

However, once the suggestion of the foundation was put before Jim, it energized him and gave him something to work on and he immediately came home and put pen to paper and talked about what he wanted to do. Jim realized very quickly that through his battle and his determination, someone else would look at their life a little differently as a result.

Fight. Persevere. Don't quit. That is the way to fill your life with special moments.

That is why Jimmy V never gave up. He wanted to watch his daughters graduate from high school and walk them down the aisle and see the birth of beautiful grandchildren. That is why Jimmy never gave in. He clearly knew his purpose in life and his priorities were in order.

There is always a reason why you should keep pushing and never stop fighting.

And even for you, there is always a reason why you should not give up. There is always a reason why you should keep pushing and never stop fighting. If you look long and hard at any situation, you will be able to find that reason. That reason will motivate you and inspire you to keep going, even when times are tough. Sometimes you may have to stop for a second and think about that reason to motivate you, but everyone who has succeeded and who has done something special had a reason for doing it, and they followed that reason to the end.

Jim's cause was no different. He wanted to leave a legacy, but not just any legacy. He wanted to find the good in his own tragic situation. And with tumors all over his body and less than a year to live, he had to look deep to find that reason. But he did and he found it. He knew if he could keep going and push along, he could lay the groundwork for a special organization to fight cancer long after he was gone.

Jim said it best:

I also told you that five hundred thousand people will die this year of cancer. I also tell you that one in every four will be afflicted with this disease, and yet somehow, we seem to have put it in a little bit of the background. I want to bring it back on the front table. We need your help. I need your help. We need money for research. It may not save my life. It may save my children's lives. It may save someone you love. And ESPN has been so kind to support me in this endeavor and allow me to announce tonight, that with ESPN's support, which means what? Their money and their dollars and they're helping me—we are starting the Jimmy V Foundation for Cancer Research. And its motto is "Don't give up, don't ever give up." That's what I'm going to try to do every minute that I have left. I will thank God for the day and the moment I have. If you see me, smile and give me a hug. That's important to me too. But try if you can to support, whether it's AIDS or the cancer foundation, so that someone else might survive, might prosper, and might actually be cured of this dreaded disease. I'm going to work as hard as I can for cancer research and hopefully, maybe, we'll have some cures and some breakthroughs. I'd like to think, I'm going to fight my brains out to be back here again next year for the Arthur Ashe recipient. I want to give it next year!

Jim fought. He never gave up. At the ESPY awards each year, Jimmy is credited as having awakened endless hearts and inspired many. He was powered by a belief and a will to make a difference in the lives of others.

Unfortunately, sometimes no matter how hard you try, you still may fall short. And that is the final lesson we take from Jim and his legacy. If you never give up, even when your game falls short or you don't cross the finish line, you can hold your head high knowing you did the best you could. Stick to the big picture, no matter your personal circumstances.

If you lose in spite of your greatest efforts, someone else might win because of your voice or your relentless courage. You will at least know you stood for something and your life mattered. That is why Jimmy V will live on forever. He stood up for the underdog on and off the court.

Stick to the big picture, no matter your personal circumstances.

Even in times when you think you failed, you have succeeded more than you will ever know. While cancer took Jim's life, it was not for his lack of effort or attitude. He never gave up. He never quit trying. He dedicated his life to making sure that cancer knew he was not going to let it be undefeated for life.

Bob Valvano told me,

Look at how far we have come. We have raised millions of dollars, funded numerous grants, and sponsored hundreds of events to fight cancer research. We have done so much. And it is great how much we have accomplished. But that was not Jim's dream. His dream was to cure cancer. And until we find a cure; our work is not done. Jim would commend us for all we have accomplished, but he would be the first to tell us that was not his dream and we still have work to do. That was just the spirit of Jim. He set his goals and would not stop until he reached them. And we have that same responsibility.

Jim would be the first to tell you that you can't win them all, but you have to try your hardest and you have to keep going. Only you decide when you give up. Jimmy V lost his life to cancer on April 28, 1993. But the legacy he left for us all has never been lost.

Jim lives on through his family and friends and their support for The V Foundation. Jim left us all a gift. He left us an organization that will fight and persevere and will never lose the battle against cancer. Every donation and every dollar The V Foundation raises is a credit to Jim's life and his battle. It is a credit to the millions of people who have been lost to cancer and the millions of dollars that have been raised to fight it. Jim left us one more thing as a legacy in the battle against cancer. He left us this speech. He gave us an outline and a blueprint on how to live life to its fullest. Sometimes it takes someone telling you that your days are numbered to truly gain perspective on your own life. Unfortunately for Jimmy, he received that news. But

If you lose in spite of your greatest efforts, someone else might win because of your voice or your relentless courage.

he left all of us the tools to live our lives to the fullest without receiving a wake-up call of that enormous proportion:

- Cherish Time, Treasure the Moment
- Make a Habit of Wild Enthusiasm
- Laugh, Think, and Cry
- Live the Big Picture
- Out-Dream Yourself
- Believe in Something Passionately
- Don't Ever Give Up

Every day we are alive is a blessing and an opportunity.

These are the lessons of Jimmy V. Thirty words that give us insight into a more fulfilling life. Jim's lessons are like a torch in a dark cave. They will guide us and they will fill us with warmth and light. But it is up to each one of us to take the time and think about these lessons and implement them into our own lives. Some may be easy, others not so much. But at the end of the day, they will make you a happier, more fulfilled human being.

None of us knows how long we have on this earth. Every day we are alive is a blessing and an opportunity. Live every day like it is your last and be the first to reach out to someone else and make a difference.

In the spirit of one of the greatest coaches and educators on and off the "court" of life, remember Jimmy V's lesson: no matter who your opponent is in life or the obstacles you face, "don't give up, don't ever give up." And we won't give up, because in the words of Jim's brothers Nick and Bob Valvano, "There is still more work to do."

ABOUT THE V FOUNDATION

It has been just sixteen years since The V Foundation for Cancer Research was founded by ESPN and Jim Valvano. And what significant work has been accomplished during that time! Since 1993, The V Foundation has raised more than $90 million and awarded cancer research grants in thirty-eight states and the District of Columbia. Researchers have developed their laboratories and taken their science from the labs to the clinics with the help of funds raised by The V Foundation.

The V Foundation started with the dream of Jim Valvano, the passionate and committed former NC State basketball coach and award-winning broadcaster, as he battled cancer. Wanting to see the battle through to victory, Valvano recruited friends and family to lead The V Foundation on his quest to eradicate the disease that ultimately claimed his life. With a dire need for early developmental, critical-stage grant support, The V Foundation was formed to assist the brilliant young researchers who will eventually find cures for cancer.

A relatively young organization, The V Foundation has a strong presence in the scientific community that belies its youth. The Foundation's Scientific Advisory Board, comprised of some of the top physicians and research scientists from prominent universities and cancer centers nationwide, assures that only the cancer research projects with the most potential are funded. Thus, grant recipients funded by The V Foundation have excellent reputations within the scientific community.

The V Foundation has an excellent track record for finding and funding elite young scientists. Between 1994, when the first V Scholar grants were awarded, and 2008, The V Foundation awarded 187 V Scholar grants to promising young researchers nationwide to help them establish their laboratories. Of those V Scholars, 93 percent have received additional funding and are still working in independent labs. An additional 5 percent are currently working in related research.

The V Foundation also takes great pride in its fiscal responsibility and is proud to announce that it gives 100 percent of all new direct cash donations and net event proceeds to cancer research and related programs. Recognized for its prudent fiscal management, The V Foundation has earned a top four-star rating from Charity Navigator, America's largest charity evaluator, six consecutive times. Receiving a top rating from Charity Navigator indicates that The V Foundation has outperformed most of its peers in its efforts to manage and grow its finances.

Passion, friendship, and commitment: these themes run deep in The V Foundation. We ask you to join us. Make a donation. Get involved. Call (919) 380-9505 or 1-800-4JimmyV to join the cause, or visit our website at www.jimmyv.org.

The V Foundation awards 100 percent of all new direct cash donations and net proceeds of events directly to cancer research and related programs.

ABOUT THE AUTHORS

ABOUT JUSTIN SPIZMAN

Justin Spizman, Esq., is a former prosecutor and currently practices criminal defense and DUI law for a private law firm in Atlanta, Georgia. He is the author of *The Insider's Guide to Your First Year of Law School.* A die-hard sports fan and dedicated fan of Jim Valvano, Justin has lived by Jim's words of wisdom in The Speech. Justin spends his free time with his wife Jaime, playing basketball, and watching sports with their trusted dog Guinness by their side.

ABOUT ROBYN F. SPIZMAN

Robyn Freedman Spizman is a *New York Times* bestselling author of dozens of books and a well-known television and radio personality heard nationally. A foremost gift expert, she reports on gifts that keep on giving and is the creator of TheGiftionary.com. For three decades, Robyn has appeared in the media, including frequent appearances on NBC's *Today* show and

CNN. She resides in Atlanta, Georgia, with her husband, Willy, and is the patient wife and mother of a family of devoted sports fans. Learn more about Robyn at robynspizman.com.